50

GREAT
FRO
PRAY
IONA CO

D0863608

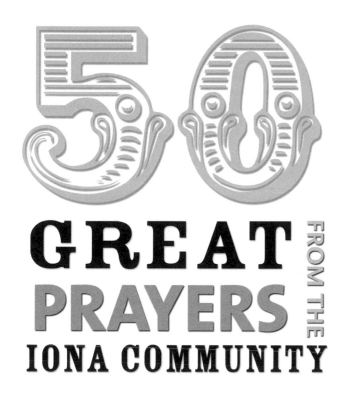

50 GREAT PRAYERS FROM THE IONA COMMUNITY

SELECTED BY NEIL PAYNTER

WILD GOOSE PUBLICATIONS

www.ionabooks.com

Prayers © the individual contributors
Compilation © 2009 Neil Paynter
First published 2009 by
Wild Goose Publications, Fourth Floor, Savoy House,
140 Sauchiehall Street, Glasgow G2 3DH, UK,
the publishing division of the Iona Community. Scottish Charity No. SCO03794.
Limited Company Reg. No. SCO96243.
ISBN 978-1-905010-62-2

The publishers gratefully acknowledge the support of the Drummond Trust,
3 Pitt Terrace, Stirling FK8 2EY in producing this book.

A catalogue record for this book is available from the British Library.

Overseas distribution
Australia: Willow Connection Pty Ltd, Unit 4A, 3–9 Kenneth Road, Manly Vale, NSW 2093
New Zealand: Pleroma, Higginson Street, Otane 4170, Central Hawkes Bay
Canada: Bayard Distribution, 10 Lower Spadina Ave., Suite 400, Toronto, Ontario M5V 2Z

Printed by Bell & Bain, Thornliebank, Glasgow

CONTENTS

INTRODUCTION

The first time I went to Iona Abbey I couldn't get in! I'd just arrived on the island to volunteer with the Iona Community for four months. I'd walked over to the Abbey from the MacLeod Centre to go to the evening service. I wanted to see what it was like – what I'd got myself into. But I couldn't even get in the door. The wild Iona wind was blowing in such a way that the door was sealed shut. At first I thought it was locked: *Typical of a church*, I thought. I pulled and pulled, and yanked on the heavy door, but couldn't get in. It seemed like a sign. A sign I wasn't welcome, that this church, too, 'wasn't for the likes of me'. *Oh well*, I thought, and walked down to the North Beach. Clouds were roiling across the huge sky, the wind was spirited – the whole landscape felt alive …

I went back the next day for the morning service, and entered the Abbey, and heard this great prayer, by Kate McIlhagga:

The shadow of the dove

When dawn's ribbon of glory around the world returns
and the earth emerges from sleep –

The shadow of the dove is seen
as she flies across moor and city.

Over the warm breast of the earth she skims,
her shadow falling on
the watcher in the tower,
the refugee in the ditch,
the weary soldier at the gate.
The shadow of peace
falls across the all-night sitting of a council,
across the tense negotiators
around a table.

The shadow of hope
is cast across the bars of a hostage cell
filling with momentary light
rooms tense with conflict,
bringing a brief respite,
a sliver of gold across the dark.

She flies untiring
across flooded fields,
across a city divided by hate and fear,
across a town wreathed in smoke.

The shadow of reconciliation,
the dove of peace
with healing in her wings,
is felt and seen and turned towards
as she makes righteousness shine

like the dawn,
the justice of her cause
like the noonday sun.

Holy Spirit of love,
bring healing, bring peace.[1]

I couldn't believe I was hearing such beautiful, relevant, poetic words in a church. It really surprised me at the time. Words that addressed justice and peace issues in the world and that touched the heart and soul. It made me curious. These words, and others like them, became a way in.

There's a line in a Dick Gaughan song about Pastor Jack Glass:

I don't know if Jack believed in God, it's kind of hard to tell
He never mentioned heaven much, he seemed obsessed by Hell.[2]

That's how I felt about the Church, before I came to Iona.

Whenever I went to church back home there was little, or nothing, in the services about the wonder and joy of life – or just the basic mystery of being alive, under the great changing sky, on the good, rich earth. And little, or nothing, about justice and peace issues. Church felt lifeless, irrelevant and smug. God was judgemental, and so was his boring son, Jesus Christ; and when he wasn't being judgemental and life-denying, he was sappy-sweet. The language was archaic, and the rhythm, stiff and dreary. There was a dusty, fusty, sometimes sterile smell coming from something, a dead religion maybe, being covered up.

What's the point of going to church if you don't find nourishment? Who would give a stone to a child who asks for bread? You might as well go find God, Christ and the Holy Spirit down on the North Beach. I was so hungry for mystery, wonder, community, challenge – Life – when I came to Iona. I was so hungry for food that would strengthen and inspire me to reach out and love.

And that's what I found in the community and worship there: Bread for body, mind and soul. Life in all its fullness. *(John 10:10)*

Not that there wasn't space for confession in the liturgy; that's essential. But you felt that sin wasn't something lodged inside you, like a bad seed; like something you were born with. Or like a pocketful of stones you hobbled through your one precious life with. Sin was more about not recognising and confessing your complicity in the injustices of the world – not acting to help feed the hungry, clothe the freezing, free the imprisoned and oppressed.

In the Iona Community's daily Act of Prayer, we say together:

With the whole church
WE AFFIRM
THAT WE ARE MADE IN GOD'S IMAGE,
BEFRIENDED BY CHRIST, EMPOWERED BY THE SPIRIT.

With people everywhere
WE AFFIRM
GOD'S GOODNESS AT THE HEART OF HUMANITY,
PLANTED MORE DEEPLY THAN ALL THAT IS WRONG.

With all creation
WE CELEBRATE
THE MIRACLE AND WONDER OF LIFE;
THE UNFOLDING PURPOSES OF GOD,
FOREVER AT WORK IN OURSELVES AND THE WORLD.[3]

When I first came to Iona, I viewed the Church the way popular culture and the media *still* views it – sin-obsessed, judgemental, life-denying, anti-nature, anti-women, anti-gay … I don't know how to spread the 'gospel of Iona', other than by trying my best to live it, and through books like this one.

It was very hard to choose only 50 prayers from the Iona Community. This anthology (like all anthologies) is subjective, I admit, although I hope I've chosen some prayers that anyone editing a collection like this would have included.

It's interesting, but not surprising, that the majority of these prayers were written by women – more evidence that the Church would have much more heart, guts and spirit – would be more fully Christ's body – if it was less male. Well, that change in the shape of the Church is slowly happening. Isn't it?

Some voices here are male, like George MacLeod's. I thought of just including passages from George's prayers, but the whole prayers are so rooted and soaring and glorious I couldn't do it; maybe didn't dare. To me, George MacLeod's prayers are of a time and will always transcend time:

In You all things consist and hang together:
The very atom is light energy,
the grass is vibrant,
the rocks pulsate.

All is in flux; turn but a stone and an angel moves ...

Not all prayers used on Iona are those that have been written down and crafted, of course. Many of the most heartfelt prayers I experienced were spoken. I remember a mother who stood up in the Abbey in a service celebrating God's gay and transgendered children. I remember open prayer during Communion at the end of each week; how those prayers in the peace and candlelight expressed so powerfully all we had shared journeying together through those weeks. It's hard to capture those prayers in a book; they exist more in the moment, more in the Book of Life.

I've avoided dividing up these prayers into sections or themes or days. There's a flow. If you're looking for a prayer for a service it won't be hard to find one; if you're travelling with the book – somewhere in the flow of life and time – you can pick it up anywhere.

I hope that these prayers find their way into your church; and I hope that you carry this book with you out in the world. I know I'll carry it with me, on the train or bus to work, on demos and marches. I'll keep it in my rucksack or coat pocket; maybe leave it at a crossroads with a fellow pilgrim and companion on the way.

May prayer feed your actions
and may your actions feed the world ...

Love,
Peace,

Neil Paynter

Biggar, Scotland
Trinity Sunday, 2009

Notes

1. From *The Green Heart of the Snowdrop*, Kate McIlhagga, Wild Goose Publications, 2004. © Donald McIlhagga. First published in *The Pattern of Our Days*, Kathy Galloway (ed), Wild Goose Publications. Written after seeing a dove banner in Brechin Cathedral.

2. Dick Gaughan is a Scottish folksinger. The lyrics quoted here are from the song 'The Devil and Pastor Jack Glass', by Dick Gaughan, from the CD *Lucky for Some*, Dick Gaughan, Greentrax, 2008 www.greentrax.com

3. This affirmation was written for the 2001 revision of the *Iona Abbey Worship Book*, by myself and the very patient and enabling Brian Woodcock, the then-Warden of Iona Abbey. The 'God's goodness' line was inspired by Philip Newell's book *Listening for the Heartbeat of God* (SPCK).

50 GREAT PRAYERS FROM THE IONA COMMUNITY

GATHER US IN

Leader: Gather us in,
          the lost and the lonely,
          the broken and breaking,
          the tired and aching,
          who long for the nourishment
          found at your feast.

ALL: GATHER US IN,
Leader: the done and the doubting,
          the wishing and wondering,
          the puzzled and pondering,
          who long for the company
          found at your feast.

ALL: GATHER US IN,
Leader: the proud and pretentious,
          the sure and superior,
          the never inferior,
          who long for the levelling
          found at your feast.

ALL: GATHER US IN,
Leader: the bright and the bustling,
          the stirrers, the shakers,
          the kind laughter makers,

who long for the deeper joys
found at your feast.

ALL: GATHER US IN,
Leader: from corner or limelight,
          from mansion or campsite,
          from fears and obsession,
          from tears and depression,
          from untold excesses,
          from treasured successes,
          to meet, to eat,
          be given a seat,
          be joined to the vine,
          be offered new wine,
          become like the least,
          be found at the feast.

ALL: GATHER US IN!

Wild Goose Resource Group

MORNING PSALM

God, I feel I could wear the day
I feel I could wear the day today
like a scarf
(But not because it's cold
'cause it's not)
I feel I could wear the day and
the wind would wrap it around and around me
I feel I could wear the day
I feel I could wear the day today
Like a scarf
and dance it
Yellow with a fringe or two of blue

Neil Paynter

TODAY

Today
may I give and receive love.

Today
may I work for justice.

Today
may I listen and pray.

Today
may I sing God's praises.

Today
may I delight in God's beauty.

Today and every day.

Ruth Burgess

CIRCUIT

I make my circuit
in the fellowship of my God,
on the machair, in the meadow,
on the cold heathery hill,
on the corner in the open,
on the chill windy dock,

to the noise of drills blasting,
to the sound of children asking.

I make my circuit
in the fellowship of my God,
in the city street
or on spring-turfed hill,
in shop-floor room
or at office desk.

God has no favourite places.
There are no special things.
All are God's and all is sacred.
I tread each day
in light or dark
in the fellowship of my God.

Be the sacred Three of glory
interwoven with our lives

until the Man who walks it with us
leads us home
through death to life.

Kate McIlhagga

YOU TAKE ME SERIOUSLY

I settle into stillness
searching
seeking
trusting your joy

My mind races
and you embrace it
wrapping me round
with wonder and grace

You wrestle with me
question me
take me seriously
I bless the honesty of your love.

Ruth Burgess

PRAYER FOR THREE VOICES

Voice 1:

God of justice, keep us silent
when the only words we have to utter
are ones of judgement, exclusion or prejudice.
Teach us to face the wounds in our own hearts

(Silence)

GOD OF JUSTICE, GIVE US POWER OF SPEECH
TO RESIST INJUSTICE, OPPRESSION AND HATE,
NOT ONLY ON OUR OWN BEHALF
BUT FOR OTHERS WHO ARE NOT HEARD.
MAKE US PEACEMAKERS AND RESTORERS OF THE STREETS.

Voice 2:

God of power, keep us silent
so that we may listen respectfully
to another person's pain
without trying to fade or fix it,
for you are present within each one of us

(Silence)

GOD OF POWER, GIVE US COURAGE
TO SHARE OUR GIFTS OF SPEECH
TO COMFORT, UPHOLD AND STRENGTHEN.
LET US BE A GLIMPSE OF YOUR LOVE TO THOSE IN NEED.

Voice 3:

God of love, in the silence of our hearts
give us words of welcome, acceptance and renewal
so that when we speak
our words come from you

(Silence)

GOD OF LOVE, GIVE US VOICES OF PRAISE
TO CELEBRATE EACH OTHER
AND THE GLORIES OF CREATION
BELIEVING THAT WE ALL LIVE WITHIN YOUR BLESSING.

Yvonne Morland

THE GLORY IN THE GREY

Almighty God, Creator:
In these last days storm has assailed us.
Greyness has enveloped and mist surrounded
our going out and our coming in.
Now again Thy glory clarifies,
Thy light lifts up our hearts to Thee,
and night falls in peace.
But through mist and storm and sunshine,
the crops have ripened here
and vines of Spain have grown.
Thy constant care in all and everywhere is manifest.

Almighty God, Redeemer:
Even as with our bodies, so also with our souls.
Redeemer, Christ:
Sunshine and storm, mist and greyness
eddy round our inner lives.
But as we trace the pattern, looking back,
we know that both darkness and light
have been of Thine ordaining
for our own soul's health.
Thy constant care in all, and everywhere,
is manifest.

Almighty God, Sustainer:
Sun behind all suns,

Soul behind all souls,
everlasting reconciler of our whole beings:
Show to us in everything we touch and in everyone we meet
the continued assurance of Thy presence round us:
lest ever we should think Thee absent.
In all created things Thou art there.
In every friend we have
the sunshine of Thy presence is shown forth.
In every enemy that seems to cross our path,
Thou art there within the cloud
to challenge us to love.
Show to us the glory in the grey.
Awake for us Thy presence in the very storm
till all our joys are seen as Thee
and all our trivial tasks emerge as priestly sacraments
in the universal temple of Thy love.

Of ourselves we cannot see this. Sure physician give us sight.
Of ourselves we cannot act. Patient lover give us love:
till every shower of rain speaks of Thy forgiveness:
till every storm assures us that we company with Thee:
and every move of light and shadow speaks of grave and
    resurrection:
to assure us that we cannot die:
Thou creating, redeeming and sustaining God.

George MacLeod

I AM TIRED, GOD

I am tired, God.
I am ready to sleep.
Let me sleep in your cradling.
Let me rest in your joy.

I give to you my worries.
I give to you my dreams.
Watch over me in blessing.
Watch over me in love.

Ruth Burgess

WEAVER

O Weaver,
shuttling the thread of glory
through the pattern of our days.
Come, bed us down
into the cloth of earth and heaven.
Come clothe us with joy.

Ruth Burgess

BECKON US, GOD

Beckon us, God
with your smile of welcome
with your strong, sure calling
BECKON US IN THE MORNING

Challenge us, God
with your love and justice
with your truth and travelling
CHALLENGE US IN THE NOONTIDE

Keep us, God
with your saints and angels
with your friends and children
KEEP US IN THE EVENING

Cradle us, God
with your songs and stories
with your hope and healing
CRADLE US TILL DAWNING
AMEN

Ruth Burgess

TOO MUCH LUGGAGE

Oh my Lord,
I am carrying too much luggage,
and it's weighing me down,
holding me back.
I worry about losing it,
but I don't need much of the stuff I'm dragging about.
It blocks up the aisles and gangways,
getting in the way,
making people cross
and wrapping itself round my ankles.
I need to learn to travel light,
but I don't know what to do with all this stuff.

Here,
you take it.
I'm leaving it with you.
Perhaps you can find a better use for it.

For who knows me better than you,
who has given me the substance of my life,
bone and marrow, patterned in my mother's womb?
You are my unfolding and my unburdening.
You are the keeper of my deepest secrets.

Kathy Galloway

GRACE FROM IONA ABBEY

Generous God,
in our world some hunger for food,
and others for meaning;
we thank you for this place and time,
where we are being fed –
sharing food for the journey,
finding companions on the Way.
Amen

Jan Sutch Pickard

IMMERSION

Incoming tide of God – cover my feet.
I yield the direction of my life to You.

Incoming tide of God – cover my knees.
I yield the rule of my life to You.

Incoming tide of God – cover my hands.
I yield the shaping of my life to You.

Incoming tide of God – cover my heart.
I yield the tending of my emotions to You.

Incoming tide of God – cover my head.
I yield my need for control to You.

Incoming tide of God – overwhelm me.
Carry me out into Your unimaginable depths.

Pat Bennett

GOD OF THE TIDES

God of the tides,
whose faithful rhythm
underlies our daily lives,
help us to keep on,
with courage and caring,
both when we are full and fulfilled
and in times of ebb and emptiness –
neap and spring tides in our lives –
within the ocean of your love.
Amen

Jan Sutch Pickard

THANKSGIVING PRAYER

Thanks be to you, God awesomely distant
thanks for the searing of shooting stars
the colours of the planets in the night sky
the space and power beyond our perceiving
which sparkles the sky of our lives with your caring.

Thanks be to you, God uncomfortably close
giving life to dead dry things –
the dance of pure stillness,
the beat of our hearts,
is your doing.

Thanks be to you, God known in a body
who blessed as he lived
who raised up our life
to be gathered as one, reaching out for the kingdom.

David Coleman

CONFESSION

O God,
your fertile earth is slowly being stripped of its riches,
OPEN OUR EYES TO SEE.

O God,
your living waters are slowly being choked with chemicals,
OPEN OUR EYES TO SEE.

O God,
your clear air is slowly being filled with pollutants,
OPEN OUR EYES TO SEE.

O God,
your creatures are slowly dying
and your people are suffering,
OPEN OUR EYES TO SEE.

God our maker, so move us by the wonder of creation,
THAT WE REPENT AND CARE MORE DEEPLY.
So move us to grieve the loss of life,
THAT WE LEARN TO CHERISH AND PROTECT YOUR WORLD.

Ali Newell

LIKE A TREE

God, help us to grow
like a garden
like a song
like a tree.

Like a great tree
Like one of those great, old trees
you meet sometimes and hug
wandering lost
or enchanted
in a deep, dark forest
in an empty field.

A great, old tree
with roots that reach down to the heart
roots that reach down but
break through the ground around the trunk and lift
as if the earth can't contain the yearning.
As if the earth shall erode and pass away and
all that shall be left in the end is Spirit.

A great, old tree
with arms that shelter and shade
and house such love.

A great, old tree
with breaks and wounds and scars
but dancing and clapping its hands.
Like a beautiful, old woman at a summer wedding.

A great, old tree still and centred
drawing on the living warm core of God
though left stripped of everything.

God, help us to grow
like a garden
like a song
like a tree.

Like one of those great, old trees
you meet sometimes
in a crowded forest
in an empty field.

Neil Paynter

WAITING

God, so much of faith is waiting
like a pregnant woman waiting in hope
like a people under siege, holding out till relief comes
like the soul lost in darkness,
unable to see even a glimmer of light
yet stumbling through the night because somewhere,
out ahead, day will surely break
God, be with us in our waiting.

Kathy Galloway

BIRTH BLESSING

As I cup my hand
around your head
   little one,
may God hold you
and keep you.

As I rock you
in my arms
   little one
may Christ shield you,
and encompass you.

As I bend to kiss your cheek
   little one
may the Spirit bless you
and encourage you.

Kate McIlhagga

MOONTIME OF THE WINTER

In the moontime of the winter,
when the sun redly rises;
in the moontime of the winter,
when the trees starkly stretch,
then, O Christ, you come:
softly as a gently falling snowflake,
with the lusty energy of a newborn boy,
the blood and pain of your coming
staining the distant horizon.

In the frost of the starlight,
when the sun gives way to moon;
in the frost of the starlight,
when the earth is turned to stone,
then, O Christ, you come:
slowly as the rhythm of the seasons,
quickly as the rush of cradling waters,
worshipped by the wise,
adored by the humble,
the ecstatic joy of your coming
heralding songs of peace.

Into the world of refugee and soldier,
the soles of your feet have touched the ground.
Into the world of banker and beggar,
the soles of your feet have touched the ground.

Into the world of Jew and Arab,
the soles of your feet have touched the ground.

Walk with us, saviour of the poor,
be a light on our way,
travel beside the weary,
fill the broken-hearted with hope
and heal the nations,
that all may walk
in the light of the glory of God.

Kate McIlhagga

GOD OF THE DISPOSSESSED

God of the dispossessed,
show me how I can be in touch
with people like Cheikh Kone (of the Ivory Coast)
who is now without a home
because he spoke the truth.

Peter Millar

GOD BEYOND BORDERS

God beyond borders
we bless you for strange places and different dreams
for the demands and diversity of a wider world
for the distance that lets us look back and re-evaluate
for new ground where broken stems can take root,
grow and blossom.
We bless you for the friendship of strangers
the richness of other cultures
and the painful gift of freedom.

BLESSED ARE YOU, GOD BEYOND BORDERS.

But if we have overlooked the exiles in our midst
heightened their exclusion by our indifference
given our permission for a climate of fear
and tolerated a culture of violence

HAVE MERCY ON US,
GOD WHO TAKES SIDE WITH JUSTICE.
CONFRONT OUR PREJUDICE
STRETCH OUR NARROWNESS
SIFT OUT OUR LAWS AND OUR LIVES
WITH THE PENETRATING INSIGHT OF YOUR SPIRIT
UNTIL GENEROSITY IS OUR ONLY MEASURE.
AMEN

Kathy Galloway

PRAYER OF THANKSGIVING FOR DIFFERENT CULTURES

Dear God, we thank you for
the richness, gifts and contributions
of different cultures
We thank you for:

Nelson Mandela
Archbishop Desmond Tutu
Aung San Suu Kyi
Mahatma Gandhi

For Ray Charles singing *Georgia* and
Little Richard singing *Tutti Frutti, Oh Rudy*
For the vocal harmonies of Ladysmith Black Mambazo

For Boogie Woogie
Be Bop
Jazz
Rap
Funk
Soul
Rock 'n' Roll

Salsa clubs
The samba
Spirituals and voices
deep and profound as wells of living water

For the heady smell of the Indian grocers
For cardamom, saffron, cloves
Jasmine, patchouli, sandalwood

For the music of accents
dance of gestures
communication of smiles
For the lined landscapes of beautiful faces

For kebabs
hummus
baklava
goulash
won ton soup
warm naan bread
tandoori
sweet and sour
rice and peas and curried goat

For Greek delicatessens
Arabic delicatessens
Italian delicatessens
For delicatessens!

For gold jewellery against black skin
the sound of reggae from the car repair shop
the pungent, sour smell of indigo-dyed cloth
the blast and blare of Notting Hill Carnival

Neil Paynter and others

LORD JESUS, IT'S GOOD TO KNOW

Lord Jesus, it's good to know
that you lived in the flesh
walked where we walk, felt what we feel,
got tired, had sore and dirty feet,
needed to eat, and think about
where the next meal was coming from.

But it's even better to know
that you enjoyed your food
the feel of perfume on your skin
the wind on your face, a child in your arms
and the good wine at the wedding.

You didn't mind when people touched you,
even those who were thought of as unclean.
You kissed people with diseases
and laid your head on your friend's shoulder.
Thank you for understanding our bodily pains and pleasures
and for valuing them.

Kathy Galloway

STORYTELLER

O storyteller,
you sit me down
and fill me with tears
and love
and laughter.

Come into my life,
and tell your story
through me.

Ruth Burgess

CHRIST OF EVERY SUFFERING HEART

Christ of every suffering heart,
bless our awakening
as we begin to
discern more and more
your presence of life
within
the tortured
the abandoned
the persecuted
the imprisoned
the exploited
the betrayed
the violated
the abused
the silenced.

Peter Millar

GO GENTLY

'Death is the last great festival on the road to freedom.' *

Go gently on your voyage, beloved.
Slip away with the ebb tide,
rejoice in a new sunrise.

May the moon make a path across the sea for you,
the Son provide a welcome.
May the earth receive you and the fire cleanse you
as you go from our love
into the presence of Love's completeness.

Kate McIlhagga

*Bonhoeffer

ALL HALLOWS

All Hallows
All Saints
All Souls
All holy

Weekly we say the words,
'We look for the
resurrection of the dead
and the life
of the world to come.'*

Those who have died
are part of us.
We name them,
we tell their stories.

The love they had for us
and we for them
is not dead
is not forgotten.

They may be alive
in another world
but we cannot
know that.

And when we die
we do not know
what will happen
to us.

We do not know
what life there is to come.

All living
All looking
All dying
All mystery

All the journey

Give me what I can grasp
and your love to keep me holy,
I will walk with you, God.

Ruth Burgess

* The Nicene Creed

LOOKING IN THE WRONG PLACES

Lord Jesus,
we are always looking for you in the wrong places;
among the good and respectable people,
when we should know you are to be found
with the poor and disreputable and outcast.

Lord Jesus,
we are always looking for you in the wrong places,
at a safe distance,
but you come so close to us,
nearer to us than breathing.

We look for you in churchy things,
but we are more likely to find you
among the pots and pans,
or around the kitchen table …

We look for you in buildings,
but you walked crowded streets,
and shorelines
and mountains …

Even now, even after Easter,
still we insist on trying to find you among the tombstones;

among long-dead dogmas,
in old, decaying fears and hurts,
in the guilts and resentments we inhabit like a coffin.

But the angel said:
Why do you look for him among the dead?
He is not here!

Lord Jesus, help us to lay down the graveclothes,
roll away the stone
and come out into life,
here and now.

We will find you,
among the living,
ahead of us, going to the Galilee we seek.
You have wrestled death to the ground,
and now there is nowhere we can go,
no darkness we can enter,
which is not God-encompassed.

Kathy Galloway

MAN IS MADE TO RISE

CHRIST ABOVE US: CHRIST BENEATH US:
CHRIST BESIDE US: CHRIST WITHIN US.
Invisible we see You, Christ above us.
With earthly eyes we see above us, clouds or sunshine, grey or bright.
But with the eye of faith, we know You reign:
> instinct in the sun ray,
> speaking in the storm,
> warming and moving all Creation, Christ above us.

We do not see all things subject unto You.
But we know that man is made to rise.
Already exalted, already honoured, even now our citizenship
is in heaven, Christ above us, invisible we see You.

Invisible we see You, Christ beneath us.
With earthly eyes we see beneath us stones and dust
and dross, fit subjects for the analyst's table.
But with the eye of faith, we know You uphold.
In You all things consist and hang together:
> The very atom is light energy,
> the grass is vibrant,
> the rocks pulsate.

All is in flux; turn but a stone and an angel moves.
Underneath are the everlasting arms.
Unknowable we know You, Christ beneath us.
Inapprehensible we know You, Christ beside us.
With earthly eyes we see men and women, exuberant or dull,
     tall or small.
But with the eye of faith, we know You dwell in each.
You are imprisoned in the lecherous, the dope fiend and
the drunk, dark in the dungeon, but You are there.

You are released, resplendent, in the loving mother,
the dutiful daughter, the passionate bride,
and in every sacrificial soul.
Inapprehensible we know You, Christ beside us.

Intangible, we touch You, Christ within us.
With earthly eyes we see ourselves, dust of the dust, earth
of the earth; fit subject, at the last, for the analyst's table.
But with the eye of faith, we know ourselves all girt
about of eternal stuff,
            our minds capable of Divinity,
            our bodies groaning, waiting for the revealing,
            our souls redeemed, renewed.
Intangible we touch You, Christ within us.

Christ above us, beneath us, beside us, within us, what need have we for temples made with hands?… save as a passing place in which to gather and adore and be abased?

We are Your living temple, by grace alone we are Your living body, the only hope of Clarity for the world – blessed be Your name for Your glorious Gospel.
IT IS SO.

George MacLeod

BEYOND EASTER

Beyond Easter
we go singing.

Having been grabbed
by resurrection
we are full of tears and laughter.

The way ahead is unknown.
It will always be like that.

But having danced in the light
we will look for glory everywhere.

Ruth Burgess

BRIGHT AND AMAZING GOD

We believe in a bright and amazing God,
who has been to the depths of despair
on our behalf;
who has risen in splendour and majesty;
who decorates the universe
with sparkling water, clear white light,
twinkling stars and sharp colours,
over and over again.

We believe that Jesus is the light of the world;
that God believes in us, and trusts us,
even though we make the same mistakes
over and over again.

We commit ourselves
to Jesus
to one another as brothers and sisters,
and to the Maker's business in the world.

God said: Let there be light.
Amen

Helen Lambie, a Resident Group member

PRAYER FOR THE CHURCH

Lord God,
whose Son was content to die
to bring new life,
have mercy on your church
which will do anything you ask,
anything at all:
except die
and be reborn.

Lord Christ,
forbid us unity
which leaves us where we are
and as we are:
welded into one company
but extracted from the battle;
engaged to be yours
but not found at your side.

Holy Spirit of God —
reach deeper than our inertia and fears:
release us into the freedom of children of God.

Ian M Fraser

COME, HOLY SPIRIT

Look at us, your church, hiding behind closed doors,
afraid of change,
anxious that even our embers will be quenched.
The world's winds have taken our breath away:
we're lost for words to tell our faith.
Come, Holy Spirit, kindle a spark in every soul,
cauterise our wounds, loosen our tongues,
warm our hearts, and – with our help –
make a cheerful bonfire of the stuff we don't need.
Change us, and then, in us,
light fires of love that will transform the world.
Come, Holy Spirit, come.

Jan Sutch Pickard

OUR FATHER

Our Father
who art also our Mother,
our Brother,
our Sister,
our Lover,
our Friend.

Thank you for being who you are
and who you will be,
world without end.
Amen

Ruth Burgess

GANNET PRAYER

God, we give you thanks
for your Holy Spirit
plummeting into our lives
like a gannet –
white wings
cleaving the grey waves –
disturbing, delighting
and defying death. Amen

Jan Sutch Pickard

SPIRIT OF LIGHTNESS AND LIFE

be with all makers and dreamers:

all who make bread
    and long to share it;
all who make music
    and long to dance;
all who make words
    and long for poetry;
all who are born in flesh
    and long to be human;
all who make love
    and trust their longing
        for life.
Amen

Joy Mead

YOU SPREAD A TABLE: PRAYER OF THANKSGIVING

Generous God,
we thank you that, time after time,
in the most surprising places,
you spread a table for us
and welcome us to the feast
of your presence.

Sometimes we feel like amazed guests
at a banquet, a great celebration;
sometimes we meet you at a kitchen table
among friends, sharing daily bread;
sometimes as children enjoying a picnic,
laughing, singing, in the sunshine;
sometimes in a dark valley, on a hard journey,
by the barbed wire, bread is broken.

Always we find nourishment;
always enough for all who come;
we see that no-one is ever turned away;
and always we are blessed by sharing –
this is the gospel feast.

Thank you for such good food,
giving strength to do your work in the world,
and for your welcome at our journey's end. Amen

Jan Sutch Pickard

THE WHOLE EARTH SHALL CRY GLORY

Almighty God, Creator:
the morning is Yours, rising into fullness.
The summer is Yours, dipping into autumn.
Eternity is Yours, dipping into time.
The vibrant grasses, the scent of flowers, the lichen on the rocks,
    the tang of seaweed,
all are Yours.
Gladly we live in this garden of Your creating.

But creation is not enough.
Always in the beauty, the foreshadowing of decay.
The lambs frolicking careless: so soon to be led off to slaughter.
Nature red and scarred as well as lush and green.
In the garden also:
always the thorn.
Creation is not enough.

Almighty God, Redeemer:
the sap of life in our bones and being is Yours,
lifting us to ecstasy.
But always in the beauty: the tang of sin, in our consciences.
The dry lichen of sins long dead, but seared upon our minds.
In the garden that is each of us, always the thorn.

Yet all are Yours as we yield them again to You.
Not only our lives that You have given are Yours:

but also our sins that You have taken.
Even our livid rebellions and putrid sins:
You have taken them all away
and nailed them to the Cross!
Our redemption is enough: and we are free.

Holy Spirit, Enlivener:
breathe on us, fill us with life anew.
In Your new creation, already upon us, breaking through, groaning
    and travailing,
but already breaking through,
breathe on us.

Till that day when night and autumn vanish:
and lambs grown sheep are no more slaughtered:
and even the thorn shall fade
and the whole earth shall cry Glory at the marriage feast
    of the Lamb.
In this new creation, already upon us,
fill us with life anew.

You are admitting us now into a wonderful communion,
the foretaste of that final feast.
Help us to put on the wedding garment of rejoicing
which is none of our fashioning
but Your gift to us alone.
By the glories of Your creation,
which we did not devise:

by the assurance of Your freeing us,
which we could not accomplish:
by the wind of Your spirit,
eddying down the centuries through these walls renewed:
whispering through our recaptured oneness,
fanning our faith to flame,
help us to put on the wedding garment.
So shall we go out into the world,
new created, new redeemed, and new enchained together:
to fight for Your kingdom
in our fallen world.

George MacLeod

YOUR KINGDOM COME, YOUR WILL BE DONE

Leader: Let us pray for the breaking in of God's kingdom
in our world today.

Lord God,
because Jesus has taught us to trust you in all things,
we hold to his word and share his plea:
ALL: YOUR KINGDOM COME, YOUR WILL BE DONE.

Leader: Where nations budget for war,
while Christ says, 'Put up your sword':
ALL: YOUR KINGDOM COME, YOUR WILL BE DONE.

Leader: Where countries waste food and covet fashion,
while Christ says, 'I was hungry … I was thirsty …':
ALL: YOUR KINGDOM COME, YOUR WILL BE DONE.

Leader: Where powerful governments
claim their policies are heaven blessed,
while scripture states
that God helps the powerless:
ALL: YOUR KINGDOM COME, YOUR WILL BE DONE.

Leader: Where Christians seek the kingdom
in the shape of their own church,
as if Christ had come to build
and not to break barriers:
ALL: YOUR KINGDOM COME, YOUR WILL BE DONE.

Leader: Where women who speak up for their dignity
are treated with scorn or contempt:

ALL: YOUR KINGDOM COME, YOUR WILL BE DONE.

Leader: Where men try hard to be tough,
because they're afraid to be tender:

ALL: YOUR KINGDOM COME, YOUR WILL BE DONE.

Leader: Where we, obsessed with being adult,
forget to become like children:

ALL: YOUR KINGDOM COME, YOUR WILL BE DONE.

Leader: Where our prayers falter,
our faith weakens,
our light grows dim:

ALL: YOUR KINGDOM COME, YOUR WILL BE DONE.

Leader: Where Jesus Christ calls us:

ALL: YOUR KINGDOM COME, YOUR WILL BE DONE.

Leader: Lord God,
you have declared that your kingdom is among us.
Open our ears to hear it,
our hands to serve it,
our hearts to hold it.
This we pray in Jesus' name.

ALL: AMEN

Wild Goose Resource Group

AFTER PSALM 19

The sky does it simply, naturally
day by day by day
the sun does it joyfully
like someone in love
like a runner on the starting-line
the sky, the sun,
they just can't help themselves
no loud voices, no grand speeches
but everyone sees, and is happy with them.

Make us like that, Lord
so that our faith is not in our words but in our lives
not in what we say, but in who we are
passing on your love like an infectious laugh:
not worried, not threatening, just shining
like the sun, like a starry night,
like a lamp on a stand,
light for life –
your light for our lives.

Kathy Galloway

AFFIRMATION

We believe that God is present
in the darkness before dawn;
in the waiting and uncertainty
where fear and courage join hands,
conflict and caring link arms,
and the sun rises over barbed wire.
We believe in a with-us God
who sits down in our midst
to share our humanity.
We affirm a faith
that takes us beyond the safe place:
into action, into vulnerability
and into the streets.
We commit ourselves to work for change
and put ourselves on the line;
to bear responsibility, take risks,
live powerfully and face humiliation;
to stand with those on the edge;
to choose life
and be used by the Spirit
for God's new community of hope.
Amen

*Jan Sutch Pickard and Brian Woodcock, written after a
demonstration at Faslane nuclear submarine base*

TAKE US OUTSIDE, O CHRIST

O Christ, you are within each of us.
It is not just the interior of these walls:
it is our own inner being you have renewed.
We are your temple not made with hands.
We are your body.
If every wall should crumble, and every church decay,
we are your habitation.
Nearer are you than breathing,
closer than hands and feet.
Ours are the eyes with which you, in the mystery,
look out with compassion on the world.
Yet we bless you for this place,
for your directing of us, your redeeming of us,
and your indwelling.
Take us outside, O Christ, outside holiness,
out to where soldiers curse and nations clash
at the crossroads of the world.
So shall this building continue to be justified.
We ask it for your own name's sake.
AMEN

George MacLeod

NEW WAYS

God of our lives
you are always calling us
to follow you into the future,
inviting us to new ventures, new challenges,
new ways to care,
new ways to touch the hearts of all.
When we become fearful of the unknown, give us courage.
When we worry that we are not up to the task,
remind us that you would not call us
if you did not believe in us.

When we get tired,
or feel disappointed with the way things are going,
remind us that you can bring change and hope
out of the most difficult situations.

Kathy Galloway

PRAYER FOR THE JOURNEY

Journeying with you, Creator God,
is to journey in your world,
full of marvels and such beauty.
To glimpse eternity in sky and sea,
to feel the earth and rock beneath my feet.

Journeying with you, brother Jesus,
is to journey with your friends.
To meet and travel a while together,
then part at the crossroads,
knowing you are with us all.

Journeying with you, Holy Spirit,
is to journey with the wind.
To move to your wild music
then try to sing your song
so others may hear.

Chris Polhill

LOOK AT YOUR HANDS

Leader: Look at your hands.
        See the touch and the tenderness.
ALL: GOD'S OWN FOR THE WORLD.

Leader: Look at your feet.
        See the path and the direction.
ALL: GOD'S OWN FOR THE WORLD.

Leader: Look at your heart.
        See the fire and the love.
ALL: GOD'S OWN FOR THE WORLD.

Leader: Look at the cross.
        See God's Son and our Saviour.
ALL: GOD'S OWN FOR THE WORLD.

Leader: This is God's world.
ALL: AND WE WILL SERVE GOD IN IT.

Leader: May God bless you.
        May God keep you ever with great care
        and lead your lives with love.
ALL: MAY CHRIST'S WARM WELCOME SHINE IN OUR LIVES,
        AND PEACE IN HEART AND HOME
        PREVAIL THROUGH EVERY DAY
        TILL GREATER LIFE SHALL CALL.
        AMEN

Wild Goose Resource Group

JOURNEY BLESSING

May our journey ahead
be blessed with
God's laughter,
silences,
risks,
challenges,
healings,
questions,
promises,
protests,
answers,
tears,
solidarity,
often uncomfortable peace and
compassion-filled surprises –
perhaps all in one day.

Peter Millar

THE PEOPLE GOD CALLS BLESSED

If I'm reading it right*
the people God calls blessed
are the ones who
feed the hungry
welcome the stranger
befriend those in trouble
care for those in pain.

Not a word about
who or what they do or don't believe in,
only a description of how they live their lives.

So I ask a blessing, God,
on my friends
who cannot
or do not
believe in you.
A blessing that they are not expecting
yet one which they will recognise.
A blessing of joy, integrity and justice,
a blessing of love and life.

Ruth Burgess

* Matthew 25: 34–46

BLESSING

The blessing of Martha's welcome,
the blessing of Mary's listening;
the blessing of action,
the blessing of reflection
the blessing of a God
who is in each of these,
and in each one of us,
be with us all.
AMEN

Jan Sutch Pickard

LIVING LETTERS

May God write a message upon your heart,
bless and direct you,
then send you out
living letters of the Word.
Amen

Neil Paynter

SOURCES AND ACKNOWLEDGEMENTS

'Gather us in' – © Wild Goose Resource Group, from 'Liturgy for Holy Communion A', *A Wee Worship Book: fourth incarnation*, Wild Goose Resource Group, Wild Goose Publications, 1999.

'Morning psalm' – by Neil Paynter, from *A Book of Blessings: and how to write your own*, Ruth Burgess, Wild Goose Publications, 2001.

'Today' – by Ruth Burgess, from *Bare Feet and Buttercups: resources for Ordinary Time – Trinity Sunday to the Feast of the Transfiguration*, Ruth Burgess, Wild Goose Publications, 2008.

'Circuit' – by Kate Mcllhagga, from *The Green Heart of the Snowdrop*, Wild Goose Publications, 2004 © Donald Mcllhagga.

'You take me seriously' – by Ruth Burgess, from *Friends & Enemies: a book of short prayers and some ways to write your own*, Ruth Burgess, Wild Goose Publications, 2004.

'Prayer for three voices' – by Yvonne Morland, from *Praying for the Dawn: a resource book on the ministry of healing*, Ruth Burgess and Kathy Galloway (eds), Wild Goose Publications, 2000.

'The glory in the grey' – by George MacLeod, from *The Whole Earth Shall Cry Glory: Iona Prayers*, George MacLeod, Wild Goose Publications, 1985, 2007 © Iona Community.

'I am tired, God' – by Ruth Burgess, from *Bare Feet and Buttercups: resources for Ordinary Time – Trinity Sunday to the Feast of the Transfiguration*, Ruth Burgess, Wild Goose Publications, 2008.

'Weaver' – by Ruth Burgess, from *Acorns and Archangels: resources for Ordinary Time – The Feast of the Transfiguration to All Hallows*, Ruth Burgess, Wild Goose Publications, 2009.

'Beckon us, God' – by Ruth Burgess, from *Praying for the Dawn: a resource book on the ministry of healing*, Ruth Burgess and Kathy Galloway (eds), Wild Goose Publications, 2000.

'Too much luggage' – by Kathy Galloway, from *Talking to the Bones: poems, prayers and meditations*, Kathy Galloway, SPCK, 1996. Used by permission of Kathy Galloway.

'Grace from Iona Abbey' – © Jan Sutch Pickard.

'Immersion' – by Pat Bennett, from *Friends & Enemies: a book of short prayers and some ways to write your own*, Ruth Burgess, Wild Goose Publications, 2004.

'God of the tides' – © Jan Sutch Pickard.

'Thanksgiving prayer' – by David Coleman, from *The Pattern of Our Days: liturgies and resources for worship from the Iona Community*, Kathy Galloway, Wild Goose Publications, 1996.

'Confession' – by Ali Newell, from *Iona Abbey Worship Book,* Wild Goose Publications, 2001 © Iona Community.

'Like a tree' – by Neil Paynter, from *Gathered and Scattered: readings and prayers from the Iona Community*, Neil Paynter (ed), Wild Goose Publications, 2007.

'Waiting' – by Kathy Galloway, from *The Pattern of Our Days: liturgies and resources for worship from the Iona Community*, Kathy Galloway, Wild Goose Publications, 1996.

'Birth blessing' – by Kate McIlhagga, from *The Green Heart of the Snowdrop*, Wild Goose Publications, 2004 © Donald McIlhagga.

'Moontime of the winter' – by Kate McIlhagga, from *The Green Heart of the Snowdrop*, Wild Goose Publications, 2004 © Donald McIlhagga.

'God of the dispossessed' – by Peter Millar, from *A Book of Blessings: and how to write your own*, Ruth Burgess, Wild Goose Publications, 2001.

'God beyond borders' – by Kathy Galloway, from *The Pattern of Our Days: liturgies and resources for worship from the Iona Community*, Kathy Galloway, Wild Goose Publications, 1996.

'Prayer of thanksgiving for different cultures' – Neil Paynter and others, from *This Is the Day: readings and meditations from the Iona Community*, Wild Goose Publications, 2002.

'Lord Jesus, it's good to know' – by Kathy Galloway, from *The Pattern of Our Days: liturgies and resources for worship from the Iona Community*, Kathy Galloway, Wild Goose Publications, 1996.

'Storyteller' – by Ruth Burgess, from *Bare Feet and Buttercups: resources for Ordinary Time – Trinity Sunday to the Feast of the Transfiguration*, Ruth Burgess, Wild Goose Publications, 2008.

'Our Father' – by Ruth Burgess, from *Bare Feet and Buttercups: resources for Ordinary Time – Trinity Sunday to the Feast of the Transfiguration*, Ruth Burgess, Wild Goose Publications, 2008.

'Gannet prayer' – © Jan Sutch Pickard. Used by permission of Jan Sutch Pickard.

'Spirit of lightness and life' – by Joy Mead, from *The One Loaf: an everyday celebration*, Joy Mead, Wild Goose Publications, 2000.

'You spread a table: prayer of thanksgiving' – © Jan Sutch Pickard, from *Methodist Prayer Handbook*. Used by permission of Jan Sutch Pickard.

'The whole earth shall cry glory' – by George MacLeod, from *The Whole Earth Shall Cry Glory: Iona Prayers*, George MacLeod, Wild Goose Publications, 1985, 2007 © Iona Community.

'Your kingdom come, your will be done' – © Wild Goose Resource Group, from 'Morning liturgy A', *A Wee Worship Book: fourth incarnation*, Wild Goose Resource Group, Wild Goose Publications, 1999.

'After Psalm 19' – by Kathy Galloway, from *The Pattern of Our Days: liturgies and resources for worship from the Iona Community*, Kathy Galloway, Wild Goose Publications, 1996.

'Affirmation' – by Jan Sutch Pickard and Brian Woodcock, from *Iona Abbey Worship Book*, Wild Goose Publications, 2001 © Iona Community.

'Take us outside, O Christ' – George MacLeod, from *Iona Abbey Worship Book*, Wild Goose Publications, 2001 © Iona Community.

'New ways' – by Kathy Galloway, from *The Pattern of Our Days: liturgies and resources for worship from the Iona Community*, Kathy Galloway, Wild Goose Publications, 1996.

'Prayer for the journey' – by Chris Polhill, from *Gathered and Scattered: readings and prayers from the Iona Community*, Neil Paynter (ed), Wild Goose Publications, 2007.

'Look at your hands' – © Wild Goose Resource Group, from *Present on Earth: worship resources on the life of Jesus*, Wild Goose Resource Group, Wild Goose Publications, 2002.

'Journey blessing' – by Peter Millar, from *Our Hearts Still Sing: daily readings*, Peter Millar, Wild Goose Publications, 2004.

'The people God calls blessed' – by Ruth Burgess, from *A Book of Blessings: and how to write your own*, Ruth Burgess, Wild Goose Publications, 2001.

'Blessing' – by Jan Sutch Pickard, from *Iona Abbey Worship Book*, Wild Goose Publications, 2001 © Iona Community.

'Living letters' – by Neil Paynter, from *Iona Abbey Worship Book*, Wild Goose Publications, 2001 © Iona Community.

WILD GOOSE PUBLICATIONS IS THE PUBLISHING HOUSE OF THE IONA COMMUNITY, WHICH IS:

- An ecumenical movement of men and women from different walks of life and different traditions in the Christian church

- Committed to the gospel of Jesus Christ, and to following where that leads, even into the unknown

- Engaged together, and with people of goodwill across the world, in acting, reflecting and praying for justice, peace and the integrity of creation

- Convinced that the inclusive community it seeks must be embodied in the community it practises

Together with its staff, the community is responsible for:

- The islands residential centres of Iona Abbey, the MacLeod Centre on Iona, and Camas Adventure Centre on the Ross of Mull

and in Glasgow:

- The administration of the Community

- Work with young people

- A publishing house, Wild Goose Publications

- Its association in the revitalising of worship with the Wild Goose Resource Group

MORE FROM WILD GOOSE PUBLICATIONS ...

Collections of meditations, reflections and resources by Neil Paynter:

This Is the Day and *Gathered & Scattered*
Readings and meditations from the Iona Community
ISBN 9781901557633 and 9781905010349

Daily readings for four months in each book – prayers, liturgies, songs, poems and articles reflecting the concerns of the Community. Can be used for group or individual reflection.

Holy Ground (with Helen Boothroyd)
Liturgies and worship resources for an engaged spirituality
ISBN 9781901557886

Liturgies and worship resources on a range of subjects and concerns – globalisation, food, water, HIV/AIDS, the environment, interfaith dialogue, the arms trade, prisoners of conscience, 20th-century martyrs, homelessness, racism, gender, living in community, youth, children, ageing, etc.

Blessed Be Our Table
Graces for mealtimes and reflections on food
ISBN:9781901557725

Invites us to recommit ourselves to act for justice each time we join in the simple sharing of a meal. It is also very much a celebration of food, of diversity, of community and sharing, of Creator and creation.

Going Home Another Way
Daily readings and resources for Christmastide
ISBN:9781905010578

Resources for Christmastide to help you hear God's Word through the commercialism of the season, the propaganda of the times; and to glimpse the sacred in the secular.

WWW.IONABOOKS.COM

The seasonal resources collection from Ruth Burgess:

Bare Feet and Buttercups
(Trinity Sunday to the Feast of the Transfiguration)
ISBN 9781905010509

Acorns and Archangels
(Feast of the Transfiguration to All Hallows')
ISBN 9781905010561

Candles and Conifers
(All Saints' and Advent)
ISBN 9781901557961

Hay and Stardust
(Christmas to Candlemas)
ISBN 9781905010004

Eggs and Ashes
(Lent and Holy Week)
ISBN 9781901557879

Fire and Bread
(Easter Day to Trinity Sunday)
ISBN 9781905010301

Covering the whole year, these six books offer prayers, responses, liturgies, songs, poems, reflections, meditations, sermons and stories, written by Iona Community members, associates, friends and others. They are suitable for use by groups and individuals.